Veedor

the condor

B. L. Walker

BLISS BOOKS
SHARON, CONNECTICUT
1995

Published by

Bliss Books
45 Herrick Road
Sharon, CT 06069
(860) 364-5135

Cover photograph by Jonathan Doster.
Illustrations by Patricia Spaulding.

Produced by

J. N. Townsend Publishing
12 Greenleaf Drive
Exeter, NH 03833
(603) 778-9883
(800) 333-9883

ISBN 0-9648959-0-0

Acknowledgments

A thousand thanks to John, Martha, Robin, and Jonathan for their endearing patience through the various revisions; Patricia Spaulding for the gift of her artistic talents; Joyce O'Brien for rearranging my words in their correct order; Roger Egan, Nancy Heiser, Beri Greenwald, Rita Citrin, Bob Casey, Kathleen Thompson, and Sue Berkman for the nuts and bolts; Bill Gregory for being a beacon; all the friends who showered me with continual support; and Jeremy Townsend, whose enthusiasm, know-how, and wise counsel provided the wind under Veedor's wings to make this book fly.

For Dolly

Pachacámac

A Bolivian folk tale, adapted by Nikki Hu and Guy VanDuser

This happened long ago, soon after the Earth began. The birds in Bolivia wanted a king, but could not agree on who it should be. They argued and quarreled until the leaves in the trees grew tired of listening. At last the wisest bird spoke:

"Let Pachacámac, the great King of the Earth, decide."

So the birds all cried out to Pachacámac, who heard them and said:

"The one who can fly nearest to the sun, where my Golden Palace is, shall truly become King of the Birds."

Then all the birds rose into the sky in a great cloud of colors; so many that the Sun could not be seen. Upwards they flew, and as they rose higher, their numbers grew fewer.

Finally, only three remained, circling higher and higher in the great blue heaven—the keen Hawk, the fearless Eagle, and the majestic Condor.

Soon one of the three came spiraling down—it was the Hawk, falling away from the height and the heat, as the Eagle and the Condor continued to climb.

Closer and closer to the sun they came. Now the Eagle felt the brightness and the heat. His eyes were burning and he had to shut them, and he began to drop away. The Condor saw him falling, and felt a great surge of pride.

"I must get nearer!" he cried, and kept climbing. The feathers on his head were burned, but still he flew higher. Soon his eyes glowed as red as the fire. Still he kept on.

Then suddenly a cool, sweet wind came from the brightness. The Condor had reached the Golden Palace of the Sun. And Pachacámac, the Father of All, sitting on his golden throne, said:

"Hail, great Condor, bird of the sun! Only you had the courage to come so high. You shall be King of the Birds, and I shall take your form when I visit the Earth. The highest of mountains shall be your home, and when you leave the Earth, you shall come here to me."

Veedor

the condor

John McNeely and Veedor at Grandfather Mountain, North Carolina. Photo by Hugh Morton.

What if you met a bird who stood three feet tall and had a wing span of nine and a half feet? And what if the bird ate a whole chicken every day and liked a treat of salmon heads and raw eggs on Sundays? And what if you knew it would live to be 70 or 80 years old and was worshipped by South American natives today as it has been through the centuries? John McNeely did meet one of these near mystical creatures, an Andean condor, and decided to adopt him.

During 1986 in California, John had worked with, and was inspired by, condors. Their personalities intrigued him, and he wanted to somehow show their unique qualities to the public. Since the species had evolved during a time when they had no natural enemies, condors seemed to have developed a tameness and curiosity that he found enormously appealing.

Condor history is the stuff from which legends spring. Andean condors' ancestors date back two million years. This, of course, is a mere blink of an eye on an evolutionary time scale. Condors are actually a relatively young species, like Homo Sapiens. Along with humans, they share their birth from Pleistocene times, 500,000 to 2,000,000 years ago.

South American condors were placed on the endangered species list in 1970. They are closely related to the nearly extinct California condors, most of which live in zoos. In 1987, only 27 California condors lived on planet Earth. But through successful captive breeding, that number has increased to about 100 birds. A few have been returned to the wild. Sadly, it's estimated that only approximately 1,000 Andean condors remain in the South American mountains, and that number is falling fast.

Although the Andean and California condors are two distinct species, they share the same problems and threat of extinction. Together, they are the largest flying birds in the Americas.

Condors are affectionate and generally even-tempered. Through the centuries, many false stories and legends have been passed along about their kidnapping babies, both human and animal. But it's impossible for condors to do that because their gray-speckled feet are not designed to grasp prey. Furthermore, they aren't interested in eating live animals; their diet is mostly carrion, dead or decaying flesh.

Among Native North Americans, as well as South and Central Americans, the condor has been revered, even considered a kind of god or spiritual messenger. They have served as emblems of courage and strength. Their feathers were used on weapons, medicine fans,and headdresses. They symbolized victories or courage, and denoted status within tribes. Some North American natives believed the Thunderbird, who usually took the form of an eagle or condor, caused thunder as it flew, and was perhaps the Great Spirit itself. The condor is depicted in ancient tapestries, murals, and pottery. Museums on both continents proudly display these beautiful pieces, some of which are more than 1,500 years old.

Colombia, Bolivia, Peru, Ecuador, Chile, and Argentina all claim the condor as their national bird. Many South American coins bear its image, and hundreds of condor-topped stone statues stand tall throughout the continent.

John McNeely had always disliked seeing birds in cages. In January 1988, he observed several captive Andean condors sharing the same cage at the Patuxent Wildlife Research Center "condorminium" in Laurel, Maryland. He watched the frustrated birds fly against their cages, wearing away their feathers. He sadly remembered a raven he had worked with years earlier who could not tolerate being caged and had to be set free.

An idea took hold. He knew he could give one of these birds a friendlier environment at his Connecticut preserve. He also believed it might be possible to train a condor for free-flight and to prepare it for traveling educational programs. This was no easy decision because he knew their relationship would become intense. The commitment might be compared to a marriage, except that there could be no divorce. This would truly be "till death do us part." Unlike a human child who would grow up and eventually be able to fend for himself or herself, this bird, raised out of his natural wild element, would always depend on a keeper for food and care.

So in April, John made a phone call to the Research Center, a call that would forever change both his life and that of the one bird who especially attracted his attention.

The chosen bird could not begin to know how lucky he was to be selected by this naturalist/ornithologist with impeccable credentials. After graduating with honors from Ohio State University's School of Natural Resources, John has managed wildlife preserves in Ohio, Maryland, New York, Virginia, and Connecticut. He is also a pilot who has hang-glided as a hobby, and is the first person ever to soar with a bird. In the early eighties, featured in an award-winning film, he is shown hang-gliding with a hawk, Altair. The film shows the bird pausing, mid-air, to rest on John's gloved hands, which are holding the glider's metal frame. Because of his work with captive and injured birds, he has acquired the proper state and federal permits to own a condor.

Additionally, John has worked with the U.S. Fish and Wildlife Service on a film about condors, and produced two other condor films in Peru. In 1987, in California, he filmed the capture of the last wild condor in North America. He also has experience filming hawks and eagles.

It's said that timing is everything. In 1988, the Patuxent Center's staff had been reduced because of federal budget cutbacks. The remaining staff simply did not have enough time to work with the birds individually. The condor John was particularly attracted to was born May 23, 1987, and was known only by a number. He had been separated from his parents, who were transferred to the Columbus Zoo, when he was nine months old to encourage the parents to reproduce another sibling. Had he been born in the wild, this infant would have remained with his parents for three years as they introduced him to foraging areas in the Andes Mountains.

Further, he had already imprinted on two of the staff whose daily duty was to throw him a frozen chicken. Imprinting is when a young animal adopts as a parent the first thing it sees when hatched, or, if a parent is lost, the young adopts whoever provides it with food. Thus, the condor had become irrevocably imprinted on humans. Obviously, he could never be released into the wild; he desperately needed a home. The time was right, and John was ready to provide a safe refuge.

Despite his dislike of caging birds, he had no choice but to design and build a pen 14 feet wide, 26 feet long, and 13 feet tall. Friends joined in a cage-raising party, and helped set posts and connect heavy fencing sections together with pig rings. The scene was set. The condor's new home awaited its tenant.

Bird's eye view, looking out at the world from inside his cage. Photo by Robin Brace.

Veedor

So, on a hot early July morning, John borrowed a friend's air-conditioned van and large dog kennel and drove from his New England home to Maryland to escort the condor north to his permanent residence. And by now he had a name.

"I had read lots of Inca history and research before I left for Maryland," John says. "I knew I would name the bird Veedor, which means 'overseer' in Quechua, a language spoken by mountain people of Ecuador, Peru, and Bolivia."

The first few hours of the 400-mile trip were unnerving for both travelers, but finally Veedor's curiosity came to the rescue. He began to poke around in the van's rear end, pecked at the straw matting, and to John's great relief, settled into preening.

"When I first saw him," John says, "he was not nearly as heavy, weighing about 20 pounds, and not as handsome as he's become. His coat was a muddled, fuzzy gray-brown. His black coat and white neck ruff didn't develop until about age four. During the period that his coat color deepened to black, white feathers started showing up, making him look as if he'd accidentally walked across a freshly painted floor when his wings were tight against his sides. Now when he opens his wings, the white spreads up on secondary feathers."

Veedor has a special beauty mark: one white feather on his right shoulder. His thick color of soft, white down serves him well in colder weather as he lowers or raises it at will to keep his bald neck warm. When he opens his beak to eat, his unique orange, spoonlike tongue acts like a conveyor belt to shovel food down his foot-long throat. A crinkled fleshy crest tops his featherless head. Of all condors, only the male Andean has a crest, called a caruncle,

6

John holds a medicine fan made from Veedor's feathers. (B. L. Walker)

Martha and Veedor holding hands. (Jonathan Doster)

Veedor gives Martha a hug following a winter flight. (B. L. Walker)

Robin and Veedor comparing wing spans. (Jonathan Doster)

Bird of the sun. (Jonathan Doster)

Robin demonstrating dominance. (Jonathan Doster)

Martha, Veedor, and young friends. (Jonathan Doster)

Veedor's special greeting to only Robin. (Robin Brace)

A curious Veedor investigates bluebirds' box. (Jonathan Doster)

King of the Birds. (Jonathan Doster)

A young Veedor, age two, surveys his territory. (Jonathan Doster)

Martha and Veedor sharing a dream. (Jonathan Doster)

After a long day, time to go home. (Jonathan Doster)

which helps attract a mate during courtship rituals.

Because Veedor's neck is so long, he can rotate his head over 180 degrees, which makes him look as if he has his head on backwards. Circles of muscle surrounding his ears allow him to shut out fluids, useful when he's bathing. There are no flaps (pinna) like the ones wrapped around human ears. The absence of pinna streamlines him and makes him aerodynamically efficient.

The condor is one of the world's most accurate weather barometers, with his featherless neck and head indicating the weather forecast. Veedor's skin turns yellow if stormy weather is on the way. He's acutely sensitive to low-frequency sounds and atmospheric pressure changes preceding a thunderstorm. Lightning makes him nervous. In July 1989, a tornado ripped through his home territory, devastating the region. The storm left him weak and short of breath.

His neck also changes color to reflect his moods. When he's happy, his neck is pink and less wrinkled. When he gets angry or excited, the area becomes deeply wrinkled and turns pale yellow.

Veedor's eyes are pale brown, like all male condors. Female condors' eyes are bright red. All condor eyes are exceedingly sharp, however, since birds of prey have eight times more vision cells than humans. Many of these extra cells are located in a round spot called the fovea that functions like a pair of binoculars. Nature has given these birds two fovea in each eye. Therefore, even though a vulture, eagle, or hawk might be flying so high that human eyes could not see them, they would have no trouble spotting a rabbit or other small animal on the ground.

Veedor

For the first couple of weeks, John gave his new "child" plenty of space to allow him a period of adjustment. He checked his cage area several times a day, and tried to minimize Veedor's transition shock. "I floundered for the first few months," he says, "trying techniques I'd used with falcons. They didn't work at all. Condors are so smart they refuse to be bribed with food like other birds. They're free thinkers and show tremendous strength of character.

"I knew I needed a lot of help and called the director of the nearby Millbrook (New York) School, a private high school, which has a zoo. Luckily for both Veedor and me, Martha Boll had just graduated. She had experience working with tough animals, and so was perfect for this enormous undertaking."

Martha's zoo tasks had included manipulating a sick 15-foot long Burmese python with itchy skin into a tub of Epsom salts, chasing a golden lion tamarin monkey through hallways, and sitting through geometry and Latin classes covered with llama vomit. "It was wonderful," she says with a sigh.

By a fortunate coincidence, Martha lives in the same rural community as John. From the beginning, her patience and intuition in finding the right combination of techniques for training Veedor were invaluable. She immediately adapted to becoming the second member of the V-team.

Following John's offer to join his staff, Martha's interest in science intensified. She learned that Mount Holyoke College in Massachusetts has one of the best science and biology departments of any liberal arts college in the country. And so for the next four years, Martha made the roundtrip from college to home every weekend and holiday to work with Veedor and learn firsthand about his incredible species.

Veedor

She graduated in 1992 with a degree in biology, and wrote her senior thesis, "Vulture Evolution," to demonstrate her interest in and devotion to raptors.

In the early years of training, because of Martha's limited availability, John scouted about for a third member for his team.

He remembered meeting an airplane captain at a dinner party who mentioned that his daughter, Robin Brace, like Veedor, also flew the skies, but as a flight attendant. She was a graduate of the University of New Hampshire with a degree in zoology, had interned at the London Zoo working with big cats, and had worked in Tanzania in baboon research and elephant conservation.

John invited Robin to his preserve. At their first meeting on September 6, 1989, Robin, like John and Martha before, fell in love with the big bird. By this time, he had gained five pounds and also some self-confidence.

Did she feel intimidated by his size? "Not at all," Robin says. "I've always had a serious respect for all animals. I feel very comfortable with them. I touched his head, and in a sense, quietly offered myself to him. During the next five days, we spent hours and hours together. I fed him and allowed us to get used to each other." So now, the three-member team had miraculously come together.

John and Martha fondly recall Veedor's first attempt at flying. Since he was born and raised in captivity and then relocated to New England for six months of training, he had no opportunity to learn how to fly for the first eighteen months of his life.

Veedor

Robin feeds Veedor his daily chicken. Photo by B. L. Walker.

In those first six months in Connecticut, he received daily contact with his trainers to establish trust. They spent long, quiet times of hand-feeding him, petting his head, speaking softly to him, and mimicking his size by squatting close to the ground so as to appear unthreatening to him. Finally, they thought he was ready to try flight. They were sure he could not fly away because his underdeveloped body muscles were not strong enough.

So, on Christmas Day, 1988, with the sun shimmering over fresh snow, and with Martha, her father and sister watching, John unlatched Veedor's pen door, carried him to an open field, and urged him to do what he was born to do: fly. On his first attempt, he only just managed to get off the ground. He flew low, and crashed into a white pine tree because he didn't know how to stop. But he had begun his initiation into his birthright: flight.

Martha and John ran to him, praised him for his bravery, and enjoyed one the finest presents any parent can receive: watching a child mature.

"Veedor's first flight was all the more impressive," John says, "since the Connecticut hills don't provide the same perfect conditions for flight found in his South American mountain homeland. The Andes follow the coastline of the Pacific Ocean for the length of the continent. They rise higher than the Rocky Mountains in this country and provide a perfect home for these giant birds. Condors need updrafts so they can ride the air like a glider. They have developed perfect balance between body size and wingspan. They can flap their wings but rarely do, saving energy for takeoffs and landings, for crossing an area with no updrafts, or for emergencies."

Wild condors will walk to a ridge crest and then, with one huge leap, propel themselves on outstretched wings. It's possible to hear wind whistle through their wings from a hundred yards away. They ride air currents to heights of more than 24,000 feet and can cruise at over 50 miles an hour. They fly in vast circles and descend in straight glides. Similar to an airplane's flaps, their broad tail feathers twist and turn along with primary "finger" feathers on wing tips. This allows them to "feel" the air and control their speed and direction. At first glance, it's easy to mistake a condor for a high-flying airplane.

John says, "There's something about the lifestyle of wild condors that makes them mellow. If they get fogged in with high clouds for several days, they patiently sit and wait. It's one of the many ways they prove their adaptability."

Veedor

Condors are birds of open spaces, designed for soaring, but unlike smaller birds, they have weak pectoral (chest) muscles. Therefore, even now that he's older and stronger, it's difficult for Veedor to generate enough flapping power to become airborne from his home site because of the forested, hilly terrain.

When he's flying either from his home field or during a presentation, in order for him to launch himself, he has to run hard to achieve 10 to 12 miles an hour before he reaches minimum flying speed. However, if the day is windy, he can become airborne with about half the effort. On muggy or rainy days, the exertion required is too tiring, so he is not encouraged to fly.

In the earliest days of training, one of the team's first jobs was to order a telemetry unit, which they attach to a tail feather, so they can find Veedor and return him home should he catch a nifty thermal and fly out of sight. During hunting season, an orange ribbon is added to the transmitter for extra protection from any potentially overzealous shooters.

Soon after his arrival in Connecticut, Veedor's trainers and volunteer helpers built a wooden box within his pen area that substitutes for a cave. It's five feet off the ground and resembles a tree house. It's become his bedroom. He likes to have the space kept clean, and daily oversees its housecleaning as his helpers scrape away bodily waste. During warm months, mint leaves are placed in the box to help keep down the insect population. As with humans, Veedor gets itchy and grumpy from bug bites.

Like all young birds, when Veedor is hungry, he lets his family know by leaning forward with his tail up and making circles with his wings. Once a day, he's hand-fed a chicken. Occasionally, the town highway crew will stop by with a road-killed deer.

Condors in the wild are not hunters, but rather scavengers who clean up bodies of dead animals. They are efficient eaters. The small amount of food they don't digest (bones and hair) is spit up. That's called casting a pellet. Veedor's digestive system does not tolerate vegetable matter, so that's included in his pellets.

As he pauses while eating, his crop expands. This is an organ unique to birds. It sits above his stomach and is a pouch in the esophagus where partially digested food is stored.

At times, Veedor eats ravenously, especially if it's something he really likes, such as chicken brains, raw eggs, liver, or swordfish. When he's feeding, even though he'd prefer to just gulp down the morsel, he still shows very strong affection, as he would show toward a parent, by stopping halfway through his treat, twisting his head sideways, rubbing his head against the feeder's hand, and making a quiet *whisshing* sound before he resumes his meal.

One would expect such a large bird to have a huge sound, but Veedor's voice consists of throaty whispers. John says, "When small birds sing, what they're actually doing is outlining an effective audio fence around their home territory, which allows them to safely raise their families. But condors don't need song because their territories are much more expansive than small birds and their visual communication is exceedingly highly developed."

In the wild, condors have a hierarchy, or pecking order, in which birds are ranked in order of dominance. It helps them avoid violent conflicts when

Veedor

John and Veedor having an afternoon talk.
Photos by Deborah McCarthy.

Veedor

they're selecting a mate or eating a carcass. If condors didn't have such a social system, fights could occur resulting in blindness, damaged wings, or even death. "While there is perfection in nature, violence can occur," John says. "In general, birds have worked out a variety of ways of measuring their community territory and setting up their hierarchy to avoid dire consequences."

Even though Veedor is captive, he still retains the wild instincts that make him want to be the number one bird in his pecking order. But to make it possible for humans to work with him as closely as they do, it's absolutely necessary for the trainers to be dominant.

Like any child, he constantly tests his trainers. If any one of them is away for several days, he may show displeasure by trying to bite them, or acting in a standoffish manner when they return. If he tries to bite, the trainers will have to be gently assertive and show him who's boss. They might have to approach him and fold the tall bird down to the ground so he looks, quite literally, like a sitting duck, as they wrap their arms around him, cuddling over him to express dominance, while also holding his beak closed. Or they might have to hold him upside down in their arms.

Veedor shows his aggressive side only to those he knows as his social group or family. He would not deliberately misbehave before an audience of strangers.

Allowing Veedor his freedom has payoffs. It has encouraged his personality to develop. He is sophisticated enough to hold his own, although he is sensitive to, and understands and obeys, the trainers' tones of voice and the commands "no," "special treat," "home," "water," and "hop up."

Because condors are so visually oriented, if the trainers turn their heads from side to side in rapid movements, Veedor becomes alert and immediately scans the area, ready for an evasive maneuver at any second. They have used this device to teach him a degree of caution about cars on the road surrounding the preserve.

During educational programs, the audience is always cautioned to stay in cluster groups. It's usually somebody wearing a hat, or the stray person who wanders away, (often a photographer who can't resist that one special shot), who attracts Veedor's attention and may find the bird perched on his head or shoulders.

"During one of our first times out," says John, "we were at a town park on a snowy day. Nearby was a large field, maybe 40 acres, and a lone cross-country skier was enjoying an outing. Naturally, Veedor was intrigued and buzzed the fellow who was more than slightly startled.

"Another time, Veedor was soaring at a school presentation when a turkey vulture, who hung out at a nearby garbage dump, spotted him. The vulture alerted some 35 of his buddies. Because the wind velocity matched their air speed, they formed a huge pattern of silent bodies hovering motionless over Veedor. This caught the attention of a patrolman who rushed into the schoolyard and assumed there must be something amiss, maybe a human corpse, at the school. Of course, when the 'culprit' was discovered to be a tame condor, everyone had a good laugh over the episode."

Perhaps at some level of consciousness, the vultures recognized Veedor as a relative since they are in the same general family. They are all very visually oriented, although turkey vultures are much lighter, feast on road kills, and can fly only on short flights, while condors are long-distance travelers.

Once, in front of about 100 students, Veedor spotted a jogger in a red jacket running on a track a quarter mile away. (The colors red and orange particularly attract his sharp eyes.) He swiftly flew to the runner, circled him, and made a final approach behind the frightened fellow who didn't know whether to run backwards facing Veedor, lie down in a fetal position, or climb a tree. But, when the bird heard John's urgent "Come, Veedor," he immediately returned to him and the cheering young audience.

Veedor is an excellent traveler. At the beginning of his training, he was introduced to a van containing a colossal-sized dog carrier, big enough to be

Robin and Veedor in his mobile cage. Photo by B. L. Walker.

comfortable for a Saint Bernard. The next step was drives around the nearby countryside. He thoroughly enjoyed the arrangement. In the wild, condors have several roost sites in case a sudden storm prevents their flying home. Veedor has accepted that he has two sites: his tree house and the van, his mobile cave. He seems to relish the visual stimulation of passing scenery as he bobs his head from side to side, and also the company of his family close by on long trips. And he never asks, "Aren't we there yet?"

When the group travels, the van is parked within view of sleeping quarters, with windows blacked out to allow Veedor a dark, private space. As humans do, he often suffers from insomnia on trips, although he definitely seems to enjoy the stimulation of different settings and varied audiences, making each excursion worthwhile for him.

While the van is in motion, there usually isn't much reaction from passing cars. But once, in bumper-to-bumper traffic, John noticed a mother writing a note which she handed to her child. The young girl climbed into the back seat, and held up the note asking, "Are you the condor man?"

"We had a wonderful time in a small New Hampshire community one summer evening," he says. "Our old van broke down, and we had to be towed into a local garage. Word got around quickly that a big bird was in town. So there, outside the auto body shop everybody and his cousin showed up. And Veedor gallantly obliged with a whole program even though he'd already made a guest appearance at a fair earlier on that hot day."

Veedor wants to be part of everything that's going on. "I was using a nylon scrub brush to clean his tub and noticed he kept trying to grab the brush," John says. "I pushed him away till he finally got the message, but then he began doing the same kind of motion with his feet along the edges of the tank. Also, when I'm using lopping shears on shrubbery around the preserve, he observes, then in mimic, selects a piece of brush and drags it away. It seems to give him a sense of pride to be participating."

Veedor doesn't like the noise of the lawn mower. Perhaps he imagines that John is having a struggle with the mower, so he charges at it. Of course, that's unacceptable behavior because he could hurt himself. But when the bird becomes stubborn about returning to his cage, as enticement, if the lawn mower is pulled from the barn toward the cage without the motor running, Veedor will follow, jabbing at the tires, and pulling at the starter. On three occasions, in an instant, he has ripped apart the spark plug cable. He seems to know the crucial parts of the mower to attack. He also enjoys pecking at rubber wheels and nibbling on trainers' sneakers.

"In the sandy part of his cage, he makes simple grooves with his beak," says John. "We assume it's a way of burning off energy, or trying to communicate. But the day that he printed an 'I' and a 'V' really flipped me out. Of course, it's easy to let my imagination run wild, but it was certainly an ET-like experience for me."

Veedor is now at an age when his nesting instincts are developing. By this point of maturity, if he were in the Andes, he would be helping his mate incubate an egg.

Once a male and female condor decide to mate, they stay together for life. They mature, and are able to reproduce, at age six. Thereafter, every other year, the female lays only one half-pound whitish egg, usually on a cave floor of a high cliff since wild condors don't build nests. Both parents take turns sitting on their egg until it hatches, in about two months. Because condors are very long-lived, they don't need to worry about laying hundreds of eggs during their lifetime.

Since there is no female bird in Veedor's life, he displays his courtship stance, with curved wings outstretched, to whatever is available, be it a lawn chair, tree stump, or trainers' legs. As his hormones rage, he quietly gathers sand around him, and has been observed patiently sitting on a blue ball for hours, presumably hoping it will hatch an offspring.

Because so many of the captive-bred Andean condors are closely related to him, it's unlikely that Veedor's bachelor status will change. However, should he become unhappy or frustrated at being alone, careful consideration will be given to finding him a mate. It's assumed his relationship with his human family will probably change if a female condor is introduced into his life. But until then, he is considered genetic surplus by the professionals managing captive condors and so he must continue his role as an ambassador in "exile."

Condors are devoted parents, which may explain why their young instinctively imprint quickly with adoptive parents. "That adaptability certainly has made our relationship with Veedor easier," says Martha.

When New England winters get intolerably cold for humans, it's also hard on Veedor, especially his unprotected feet. If he were living in the Andes, he would simply soar to a warm, sunny cliff, or float down to the Pacific shore. His sixth winter in Connecticut turned out to be the coldest ever recorded according to weather sources. The snow was too deep to allow him to make running takeoffs, so he became exhausted from having to flap his wings excessively. He frequently plowed into the snow, chest deep, panting. Arrangements were subsequently made to give him a warmer climate winter vacation during Connecticut's coldest months.

In general, however, Veedor prefers the cooler New England weather to those days when the temperature soars to above 70 degrees. Birds don't sweat, so given the thickness of his coat of feathers, warm, humid days cause him considerable discomfort. On a muggy day, you'll find him splashing in his tub, then stretching his wings to drip dry.

Condors are clean birds. Veedor meticulously preens several times a day. After eating, he will carefully and gracefully groom his head and body using whatever is near—sand, grass, maybe a pantleg—then wash himself in his tub. He likes to play with floating apples in the tub, and to blow bubbles in mud created from water splashed from the tub.

He's very private about bathing, and usually won't get in unless left alone. But it seems to be one of his great pleasures.

Most often, Veedor has to be coaxed into the van even though it's one of his roost sites. But at the beginning of a recent trip, he ran up the 1- by 12-foot plank into the van to avoid a drizzly rain. The V-team was going to be traveling for several days, and it was important that Veedor enjoy some good pre-trip exercise. The day was warm enough so that he wouldn't suffer from hypothermia. He did take a couple of short flights, but wasn't interested in really spreading his wings and getting soaked. He doesn't like to get wet in a downpour, probably because he doesn't know how long the rain will last and therefore how long it will take to dry out.

However, bathing in his tub is another matter because he knows he will be dry within two or three hours. He has sometimes made the mistake of taking baths on days that were too humid, or too still or cloudy, and he didn't dry off by darkness. On those occasions, he probably suffered through uncomfortably clammy nights.

Veedor is free to bathe whenever he feels the need. But, if he hasn't bathed for a while, a team member will drain some of the tub and run fresh water. That sound stimulates him to hop in. During winter months, they move the tank into a sunny spot. If it's a reasonably warm day, he'll jump right into the tub and splash around, happy as can be, amidst the snow.

Veedor's keepers spend several hours every day talking to and playing with the bird. They monitor his health carefully before taking him out of his pen so he can exercise his wings and fly through the preserve. When called by name, he usually returns to his trainers' arms, which they stretch overhead.

Veedor is highly intelligent and remembers visitors and responds to each differently by adopting various greeting postures. Perhaps he will lower one shoulder, or tilt his head at a particular angle to acknowledge someone he's met before. He has a distinct greeting for at least thirty frequent visitors to the preserve. Robin notices that when she returns from a trip, he welcomes her home by rolling circles with his wings, his particular greeting only for her. He begins that gesture even before she steps out of her car. "We feel he's offering a form of respect by recognizing individual people," she says.

He's enormously curious and likes to explore the land and inspect any changes. His sharp eye and keen memory don't miss a thing. One of his favor-

Playing with John and Martha at an Audubon festival. Photo by B. L. Walker.

ite toys is a garden hose. He pecks at it with his ivory-colored beak, tossing it around like a snake.

Or he might be found perched on a birdhouse, inhabited by tree swallows, his talons balancing on the small wooden frame, as he bends forward, peering into the tiny entrance hole.

One summer day, the tree swallows returned to find Veedor atop their home. Showing displeasure at this intrusion, the tiny birds dive-bombed him, smacking him on his head until he jumped to the ground and ran to his amused human family for protection.

Veedor

He enjoys playing games, at home and in front of audiences. Most favorite is king-of-the-mountain wherein his 28-pound body is held high over trainers' heads. Tug-of-war with a cardboard box or quilt is also a favorite pastime. He seems to know when his friends want to stop playing and voluntarily drops the object and doesn't persist.

Some days he likes to wedge his head into a glove and strut around

Veedor helicopters over John and an admiring Vermont audience. Photo by Rick Russell.

showing off his pretend crown. While exploring on the ground, he's developed a kind of Groucho Marx walk for balance. He doesn't seem to mind when visitors mimic him and join in the fun.

Robin recalls an occasion when she returned to the compound after a severe autumn storm had uprooted a white pine tree and plunged it through the wire netting covering his pen. The tree had been stuck in his space for several hours. Veedor's attitude seemed to ask: "Where have you been? Don't you see I need help cleaning up this mess?" He had to be relocated into the van while the tree was chain sawed into movable pieces. But he appeared perfectly content when the van was backed close to the activity so he could oversee the effort.

Veedor thrives in the spotlight. He seems to like being in front of audiences of children and adults as much as they thrill at being near him.

More than a quarter of a million people have had the pleasure of Veedor's company. He's been invited to appear at such gatherings as a national Boy Scout jamboree, at the National Zoo in Washington, D.C., at National Audubon and international peace festivals, and before an information gathering hearing of a congressional subcommittee on environmental and natural resources.

At the Capitol, Veedor had his first ride in an elevator. When he and his trainers arrived on the third floor, he stepped out of the confined space, fluffed up his feathers, walked into the hearing room, and completely captivated the legislators as he strode before them on a blue carpet.

When the team returned to the northeast, a Boston-based dancer, Nikki Hu, was so impressed with Veedor that she choreographed a piece called, "I Want to Dance With a Condor Before They Become Extinct," in which Veedor actually participated.

Choreographer Nikki Hu performs a lift with Veedor, her most unusual dance partner to date. Photo by Guy Van Duser.

Veedor

Musician Paul Winter marvels at two-year-old Veedor.
Photo by Jonathan Doster.

Veedor is frequently included as special guest at the Blessing of Animals held at the world's largest gothic-style cathedral, Saint John the Divine in New York City. On those occasions, artist-in-residence Paul Winter and his Consort weave music together on widely diverse instruments from around the world. The music uses whale songs, wolf howls, and bird calls from some of our endangered friends.

Paul Winter invited Veedor to be part of an Earth Mass at the Yale Summer Music School in Norfolk, Connecticut. At the conclusion of the ceremony, Veedor brought up the rear of the menagerie, riding high down the center aisle of the concert hall on Martha's arms, stretched overhead. In front of a sold-out audience, he turned his head to look at the crowd and seemed to ask, "You want to see awesome? I'll show you awesome." Whereupon he spread his glorious wings and brought a collective sigh of oohs and aahs from everyone present. Some were seen to wipe away tears in that profound moment.

That same summer, the V-team appeared at an international peace festival in New York State. When the South American community heard the condor would be present, busloads of Peruvians, Colombians, and Ecuadorians living in the New York City area made the trip to see a bird sacred to their culture.

Tragically, today's world is fraught with dangers for condors, most caused by humans. Their eggs are stolen, or the condors are killed because uninformed farmers consider them a threat to livestock and deliberately poison or shoot them. Some birds have accidentally flown into electric power lines. Many have ingested bullets from carcasses and died of lead poisoning or from drinking antifreeze. Additionally, thousands of acres of rangeland on which they forage have been developed into agricultural or human habitat space, thus squeezing their foraging territory into smaller and smaller parcels.

Condors are just one of the world's many endangered species. As more and more species become extinct because of rapaciousness and encroachment on their breeding territory, the world loses important resources.

Veedor

In the overall scheme of life, scavengers are valuable and necessary.
They help keep our surroundings clean. In addition, the biology of birds makes
them immune to rabies, harmful bacteria and viruses, and other dread disease.
By eating dead animal material, which is frequently putrid, condors help
control the spread of disease by acting as a kind of biological filter.

Some of today's diseases are breeding so fast and becoming so virulent
and drug-resistant that scientists can't develop cures fast enough. Therefore,
medical research might do well to study birds to try to unlock their genetic
secrets of immunity, or to learn why, especially in the case of condors, they live
longer than many humans.

Someone you know may ask, "What difference does it make that we're
losing plants and animals at a dangerous rate?"

John responds: "First there is the humane reason. Each creature has as
much right to live on earth as we humans do. But also, each living animal or
plant is part of the food chain, which we are thoughtlessly disrupting.

"For example, losing any of a number of plants could mean starvation
for certain birds and insects who keep food crop pests in check. And what if
we accidentally destroyed the very plant or animal that held the secret to a
cure for AIDS, cancer, tuberculosis, or any unnamed disease on the horizon?
Therefore, it's to our advantage to learn about human overpopulation, careless
destruction of natural habitat, and causes of water and air pollution."

John points out that "most of earth's creatures, other than humans,
depend solely on the sun's energy to sustain life: for food, warmth, and transportation. Condors, for example, can coast hundreds of miles on our sun's
energy, which forms the wind or thermal updrafts.

Veedor

"Humans, on the other hand," John notes, "depend on fossil fuels derived from plants that lived 300 million years ago for transportation, light, and heating or cooling our homes. Burning these fossil fuels uses up the earth's resources and also pollutes air and water.

"So you might conclude," he says ironically, "that it's not the condors who are endangered. They have perfected a pure-cycle way of life. They neither pollute nor waste. Rather, we humans are the ones creeping further out on the endangered species limb as we gobble up non-renewable fuels, poison oceans, lakes, rivers, and streams, and cut down valuable rain forests."

Further, Robin reminds us: "Through ignorance and fear, we've greatly reduced the population of bears, mountain lions, wolves, and tigers. Now add condors to that list. People don't stop to realize that what 'civilization' has done is an indicator of what will happen in the future—fewer and fewer species, thus making the chain weaker. Should the unthinkable happen and all condors become extinct, humanity will have lost an important link to Mother Earth's past."

And Martha sums it up: "We know we will always have to lead Veedor into his shelter at day's end, even though we wish he could just sail off toward the moon. But, we're doing the best we can. We hope that as we spread the word, more of his cousins will fly free."

Thus John McNeely's vision has become reality. He has saved the life of a member of an important species. John and his V-team teach us awareness of, and respect for, all of earth's families.

So hail, Great Veedor, the world's only free-flying, captive Andean condor, and a majestic ambassador for condors in the wild.

More About Condors...

Condors are a type of New World vulture belonging to the family Cathartidae. They probably descend from the same line as storks, unlike Old World vultures (those of southern Europe, Asia, and Africa) which share ancestry with eagles and hawks. They are two unrelated types of birds that look alike because they developed the same adaptations for remarkably similar ways of life. All are called raptors, meaning birds of prey.

Raptors

Order Falconiformes — Diurnal (daytime flight)
   Suborder family Cathartidae (New World vultures)
   Suborder family Acciptres (hawks, eagles, ospreys, kites, and Old World vultures)
   Suborder family Sagittorii (Secretarybird)
   Suborder family Falconae (falcons)
Order Strigiformes — Nocturnal (night flight) — all owls.

Dreamscapes III

Martha Boll

I've flown with condors in my dreams
To castles in the air—
Above blue gossamer wind gardens
Spun by wistful seraphim—
With air breathing us heavenward
We see the Earth becoming round—
Distant—
Her edges hemmed in ebony infinity—

The darkness is like coming home
And dancing with the moon—
Beyond some necromantic desire
Finally fulfilled—

Photo by Jonathan Doster.

We've soared past Nowhere
Into Now-Here—
Shattering the incomplete visions
Of archaic utopias
And the anachronistic chimera
Of past and future
With one sweep of our wings—

We've rousted finally
From our moral somnivolation
To join the cosmic collective
Consciousness—
The Ten Thousand, the Way, the One—
We peruse the flora and fauna
Of another universe—
And weave laurels of stellar foliage
To celebrate
The constant creation of creation
From embryonic solar systems—

Galaxies between us flow
From fingertip to feathertip
As we witness our endless rebirths
From the dark wombs of imploded stars—
And we are light quietly glowing
Steadily growing and moving—
Stirring the darkness
In gentle whirlpools
Of change and fancy—
Keeping it fertile
For reasons of beauty—
Spilling over—
Forward into glory—

Glossary

Carrion	Dead or decaying flesh
Caruncle	A fleshy skin outgrowth on a bird's head
Casting a pellet	Spitting up undigested food (hair, bones)
Crop	A pouch in the esophagus of birds in which food is stored or partially digested
Fossil fuel	Oil, coal, or gas formed from plant material that lived millions of years ago and is now stored in the earth's crust
Fovea	A round spot in the eye's retina; the area of most distinct vision
Imprint	Acceptance of another animal or human as parent
New World	North and South America
Old World	Africa, Asia, and Europe
Ornithologist	An expert on birds
Pectorals	Chest muscles
Pinna	External part of the ear
Pleistocene	Geologic era 500,000 to 2,000,000 years ago
Putrid	Decomposed, foul-smelling, rotted organic matter
Raptor	A bird of prey
Scavenger	An animal that feeds on carrion or other decaying organic matter
Talon	The claw of a bird of prey; toenail
Thermal	Air updraft caused by heat
Virulent	Extremely poisonous, toxic

Bibliography

Arnold, Caroline. *On the Brink of Extinction*. San Diego: Harcourt, Brace, Jovanovich, 1993.

Cadieux, Charles. *These Are the Endangered*. Washington, D.C.: Stone Wall Press, 1981.

Ehrlich, Paul and Anne. *Extinction: The Causes and Consequences of the Disappearance of Species*. New York: Random House, 1981.

Halle, Louis J. *The Appreciation of Birds*. Baltimore, MD: Johns Hopkins University Press, 1989.

Lampton, Christopher. *Endangered Species*. New York: Franklin Watts, 1988.

McGahan, Jerry and Libby. *The Condor, Soaring Spirit of The Andes*. National Geographic, May, 1971.

Newton, Ian (consulting editor). *Birds of Prey*. New York: Facts on File, 1990.

Schorsch, Nancy T. *Saving the Condor*. Danbury, CT: Franklin Watts, 1991.

About The Author

B. L. Walker was born and raised in Western Pennsylvania, but has lived most of her life in a cottage in the woods of Northwestern Connecticut with Cleo, her gray tabby cat. Promoting the arts, behind the scenes and onstage, gives her great satisfaction. Having published both fiction and nonfiction in magazines and newspapers, she has turned her writing talent to scripting movies. Reviewing stage plays for radio fills many hours when she isn't playing piano or ballroom dancing.

About The Producer

J. N. Townsend Publishing is devoted to producing, publishing, and selling works of literature about living with animals that will promote humane and respectful treatment of animals and the world we share.